NICOLE BEHARIE:

Hollywood Icon And Child Actress

Mary J. Coyne

TABLE OF CONTENTS

INTRODUCTION

One of the most gifted and well-liked actors of her generation is Nicole Beharie. She has acted in several well-known films and television episodes, such as Miss Juneteenth, Underground, and Sleepy Hollow. Beharie is renowned for her affecting performances, and she has won countless accolades and been nominated for many more.

We will examine Nicole Beharie's biography and prominent career in this book. We shall find out about her modest beginnings, the ascent to fame, and the difficulties she has encountered. Additionally, some of her most notable performances will be examined in greater detail, and Beharie herself will speak about her acting philosophy and her hopes for the future.

Beharie is a role model for a lot of people, and her story merits being shared. She serves as an inspiration for budding performers, speaks out for inclusiveness and reform in the entertainment sector, and serves as a timely reminder that anything is possible if you put in the necessary effort and pursue your goals.

This book is for everyone who wants to learn more about Nicole Beharie's life and work and who wants to be motivated by her perseverance and achievement. It is a tale about the durability of the human spirit, the value of hard effort, and the influence of dreams.

Chapter 1: Who Is NICOLE BEHARIE

American actress Nicole Beharie is one of them. She's stylishly dressed and honored for her leading performances in the WGN America literal drama Underground and the Fox TV series Sleepy Hollow. She has also acted in flicks including American Violet and Shame. On October 3, 1985, Beharie was born in West Palm Beach, Florida. She made her amusement debut when she was a little child by sharing in indigenous theater plays. She graduated in 2007 from the Juilliard School, where she studied. Following her scale from Juilliard, Beharie started to make appearances in supporting places on series including The Good woman and Law & Order Special Victims Unit. She was cast in a supporting part in the movie American Violet in 2011. She also made an appearance in Steve McQueen's 2011 film Shame. In the 2013 TV season of the Fox series Sleepy Hollow, Beharie was given the title part of Abbie

Mills. The TV program featured a contemporary adaptation of the well- known Washington Irving tale" The Legend of Sleepy Hollow." Beharie's performance on the show was praised by the critics, and she was nominated for multiple prizes as a result. The third season of Sleepy Hollow saw Beharie leave. She quit without giving any sanctioned reason, still, it was bruited that she did so because of disagreements with the show's directors regarding her cultural vision. Beharie acted in the literal drama Underground on WGN America after leaving Sleepy Hollow. The drama centers on a gang of slaves who compass a perilous break from slavery. Beharie's performance drew praise from the critics formerly more, and she was nominated for multiple prizes for her work on the program. Beharie has likewise had important appearances in 42, Black Mirror, and Miss Juneteenth, among other well- known flicks and TV programs. She's now in the process of rephotographing the So Help Me Todd TV series. Beharie is a blessed and adaptable actress who has acted in several well- known flicks and TV programs. She's famed for her largely lauded places in the flicks Underground and Sleepy

Hollow. Beharie is a strong exponent of addition and diversity in the entertainment sector.

1.1 Early Life

On January 3, 1985, in West Palm Beach, Florida, Nicole Beharie was born. She was raised in the United Kingdom, Jamaica, Nigeria, and Panama since her father worked for the US Foreign Service. She attended Orangeburg Wilkinson High School in Orangeburg, South Carolina, and graduated from the public domestic South Carolina Governor's School for the trades & Humanities in 2003. Beharie made her amusement debut when she was a little child by sharing in indigenous theater plays. At the British American Drama Academy in London, she also studied amusement. Beharie was accepted to the Juilliard School in New York City after she completed high academy, where she studied acting from 2003 to 2007. Beharie shared in several pupil plays as a pupil at Juilliard, including Romeo and Juliet, A Midsummer Night's Dream, and The Crucible. The Royal Shakespeare Company in Stratford- upon- Avon, England, ate her as a pupil thanks to the coveted Shakespeare Scholarship that she also won. Following her scale from Juilliard, Beharie started to make appearances in supporting places on series including The Good woman and Law & Order Special Victims Unit. In the 2008 movie American Violet, where she played a youthful lady incorrectly indicted of a crime, she also made her amusement debut. Beharie's early times were characterized by her love of acting and her will to succeed. She crushed several obstacles, including growing up abroad and enrolling at a prominent performing trades council. Beharie's early guests helped to shape her into the talented and successful actress she's moment.

In an interview, Beharie said " I think my upbringing has made me a more empathetic and compassionate person.It's also made me more curious about the world and about the different people in it. I suppose that is important for an actress, to be suitable to understand and connect with people from all walks of life."

Beharie's early life helped to fester her into the accomplished actress she's moment. She crushed several obstacles, similar as growing up abroad and attending a prominent performing trades council. Beharie's early guests have given her a profound sapience into the mortal condition and have enabled her to approach her work from a distinctive standpoint.

1.2 Background

Nicole Beharie is a cultivated American entertainer known for her flexible exhibitions in front of an audience and screen. Here is an outline of her experience:

1. Early Life: Nicole Beharie was brought into the world on January 3, 1985, in West Palm Ocean side, Florida, USA.

2. Instructive Pursuits: She sought her schooling at the South Carolina Lead Representative's School for Human Expression and Humanities, a renowned expressions secondary school. Afterward, she went to the Julliard School's Theatrics Division, one of the world's driving performing expressions centers, where she leveled up her acting abilities.

3. Early Career: Beharie's vocation started on the stage, where she earned respect for her uncommon abilities to act. She showed up in a few outstanding dramatic creations, exhibiting her ability in both traditional and contemporary jobs.

4. Film Debut: In 2008, Beharie made her film debut with a little job in the widely praised film "American Violet," where she imparted the screen to Alfre Woodard.

5. Advancement Role: Beharie's cutting-edge job came in 2011 when she featured as Abbie Plants in the famous TV series "Sleepy Hollow." Her presentation gathered boundless recognition and laid out her as a rising star in media outlets.

6. Remarkable Film Roles: Beharie has been adulated for her work in movies, for example, "Disgrace" (2011) close by Michael Fassbender, "42" (2013) in which she depicted Rachel Robinson, and "Miss Juneteenth" (2020) where she played the lead job of Turquoise Jones.

7. Grants and Recognitions: All through her vocation, Beharie has gotten basic approval for her exhibitions. She has been selected for different honors, including a NAACP Picture Grant for Exceptional Entertainer in a Movie for her part in "42."

8. Promotion for Diversity: Beharie is known for her backing of variety and inclusivity in media outlets. She

has revolted against the significance of bona fide portrayal and has been a functioning voice for change.

9. Individual Interests: While her expert life is irrefutably factual, Beharie will in general keep her own life somewhat hidden. Her emphasis remains principally on her specialty and her backing work.

Nicole Beharie's experience is portrayed by a devotion to her art, a guarantee to genuine narrating, and an energy for supporting more prominent variety and inclusivity in media outlets. Her ability and backing work keep on having a beneficial outcome on both the imaginative and social scene.

Chapter 2: Acting Career Beginnings

Nicole Beharie started her acting profession early on, showing up in nearby theater productions. She additionally took acting classes at the English American Show Foundation in London.

After moving on from secondary school, Beharie was accepted into the Juilliard School in New York City, where she concentrated on acting from 2003 to 2007. While at Juilliard, she showed up in a few understudy creations, including Romeo and Juliet, A Midsummer Night's Fantasy, and The Cauldron. She likewise got the esteemed Shakespeare Grant, which permitted her to learn at the Imperial Shakespeare Organization in Stratford-upon-Avon, Britain.

In the wake of moving on from Juilliard, Beharie started showing up in visitor jobs on TV programs like

Regulation and Request: Extraordinary Casualties Unit and The Great Spouse. She likewise made her film debut in the 2008 film American Violet, in which she played a young lady who is erroneously blamed for wrong doing.

Beharie's initial acting experience was priceless. She figured out how to act before a live crowd and how to function with different entertainers and chiefs. She likewise acquired insight into a wide range of jobs, from Shakespeare to contemporary TV.

Beharie's initial acting experience assisted her with planning for her breakout job in the Fox TV series Lethargic Empty. She had the option to draw on her preparation and experience to make a complex and nuanced character. Beharie's presentation in Tired Empty was widely praised, and she got a few honors selections for her work.

Beharie's initial acting experience is a motivation for entertainers. She showed that it is feasible to make progress in media outlets, regardless of whether you have a ton of involvement. She is a good example for youngsters who are chasing after their fantasies.

2.1 Notable Projects In Early Career

During the beginning phases of her vocation, Nicole Beharie earned respect for her excellent acting abilities, both in front of an audience and on screen. Here are a few prominent undertakings from her initial vocation:

1. American Violet" (2008): This film denoted Beharie's presentation, where she assumed a supporting part close by Alfre Woodard. The film, given a genuine story, got basic recognition for its strong depiction of civil rights issues.

2. The Express" (2008): Beharie showed up in this true-to-life sports show, depicting Sarah Ward, the old flame of football player Ernie Davis (played by Ransack Brown). The film recounts the account of Davis, the first African American to win the Heisman Prize.

3. American Violet" (Stage Production): Before the film transformation, Beharie had acted in a phase creation of "American Violet," displaying her acting ability in a live dramatic setting.

4. A Liberated Individual of Variety" (2010): Beharie's stage work kept on collecting consideration, and she showed up in this verifiable play by John Guare, which debuted on Broadway.

5. My Last Day Without You" (2011): Beharie played the lead job in this heartfelt show, where she depicts a young lady who gets an opportunity to experience a German money manager. The film investigated subjects of affection, culture, and self-improvement.

6. The Great Spouse" (2011): Beharie made a visitor appearance in this well-known legitimate dramatization series, exhibiting her flexibility as an entertainer in an alternate medium.

7. Shame(2011): This movie, coordinated by Steve McQueen and featuring Michael Fassbender, highlighted Beharie in a supporting job. Her presentation was widely praised, adding to the film's prosperity.

These early tasks laid out Nicole Beharie as a gifted entertainer with a solid presence both on screen and in front of an audience. Her capacity to handle different jobs of different sorts set her to proceed with progress in media outlets.

2.2 Her Leading-edge Job In American Violet

Nicole Beharie's leading-edge job was in the 2008 film American Violet. She played Dee Roberts, a youthful African American lady who is dishonestly blamed for medication wrongdoing and captured in a police strike. The film depends on a genuine story, and Beharie's exhibition was widely praised.

Beharie was commended for her naturalism and her capacity to convey the profound intricacy of her personality. She likewise got acclaim for her actual presentation, as she needed to figure out how to play the drums for the job.

American Violet was a basic and business achievement, and it assisted with making Beharie famous. She was assigned a few honors for her presentation, including the Free Soul Grant for Best Female Lead.

Beharie's cutting-edge job in American Violet was a huge second in her profession. It showed that she was a capable and flexible entertainer who could deal with a difficult job with elegance and expertise. The film additionally assisted with bringing issues to light of the issue of racial profiling and the mass detainment of African Americans.

American Violet is a significant film, and Nicole Beharie's presentation is something that works everything out such that extraordinary. She gave a strong and moving presentation that resonated with crowds. Beharie's cutting-edge job in American Violet is a sign of her ability and her devotion to her specialty.

2.3 Sleepy Hollow

Sleepy Hollow is an otherworldly show TV series that was broadcast on Fox from 2013 to 2017. The show depends on the 1820 brief tale "The Legend of Sleepy Hollow " by Washington Irving.

The series follows Ichabod Crane (Tom Mison), an English American trooper and spy, who is revived 250 years after his passing and collaborates with Abbie Factories (Nicole Beharie), a nearby police lieutenant, to stop the powers of fiendish that are compromising the town of sleepy Hollow, New York.

Beharie's presentation as Abbie Plants was widely praised. She was adulated for her solidarity, insight, and weakness. Plants was a mind-boggling and balanced character, and Beharie rejuvenated her with subtlety and profundity.

Sleepy Hollow was a well-known show, and it circulated for four seasons. It was dropped in 2017 due to declining evaluations. Be that as it may, the show stays a clique #1, and Beharie's exhibition as Abbie Factories is still affectionately recollected by fans.

Sleepy Hollow was a huge part of Beharie's profession. It was her initial feature job on a significant TV series, and it assisted with making her a commonly recognized name. The show likewise offered her the chance to work with a gifted cast and team and to investigate perplexing and testing subjects.

Beharie's exhibition in Sleepy Hollow is quite possibly her best. She rejuvenated Abbie Mills with insight, strength, and weakness. Factories were a perplexing balanced character. Beharie made her interesting and credible.

Sleepy Hollow is a show that merits watching, and Beharie's exhibition is one reason why. She is a capable entertainer who should be perceived for her work.

2.4 Beharie's Giving A Role as Abbie Mills

Nicole Beharie's given role as Abbie Mills in the TV series "Sleepy Hollow " was a significant second in her profession. In 2013, Beharie got the lead job in the FOX Otherworldly show, Not Set in Stone, and I was able to be Lieutenant Abbie Mills. This marked a huge leap forward for Beharie, as it put her at the front of a high-profile network TV program.

Beharie's depiction of Abbie Mills was broadly commended for its profundity, validity, and how she rejuvenated an engaging and enabled character. Her science with co-star Tom Mison, who played Ichabod Crane, added to the show's prosperity. Beharie's exhibition procured her basic recognition and a dedicated fan following.

Through her job as Abbie Mills, Beharie exhibited her acting ability as well as turned into an image of portrayal and variety in media outlets. Her presence as a solid, Black female lead was a critical stage towards more extensive inclusivity in TV.

By and large, Nicole Beharie's role as Abbie Mills remains a milestone second in her profession, hardening her as a capable and compelling figure in the realm of TV.

Chapter 3:Critical Acclaim And Recognition

The reviewers praised Nicole Beharie's portrayal of Abbie Mills in Sleepy Hollow. She was acclaimed for her brilliance, vulnerability, and strength. Mills was a complicated and complete character, and Beharie gave her life with complexity and subtlety.

Numerous awards were given in recognition of Beharie's performance. She received three NAACP Image Award nominations for Outstanding Actress in a Drama Series, and she took home the prize in 2014. She was also a finalist for the Saturn Award for Best Actress in Television and the BET Award for Best Actress.

Beharie received recognition for both her performance and her particular accomplishments. Many reviewers stated that Beharie was the show's "heart and soul" and that her performance was one of the elements that set the production apart.

The portrayal of Abbie Mills by Beharie is one of her greatest. She gave the role depth by balancing brilliance, toughness, and vulnerability. Beharie gave Mills a complete, multidimensional personality that helped readers identify with and believe in her.

The honors Beharie has received are evidence of her brilliance and commitment to her field. She is an accomplished actress who merits praise for her work.

Chapter 4: The Demand And Triumph of Show Biz

The Demands and Triumphs of Showbiz" in Nicole Beharie's career shows the struggles and achievements she encountered in the entertainment industry.

Exploring the requests of showbiz requires strength, commitment, and a solid hard-working attitude. Beharie, all through her vocation, showed an unfaltering obligation to her specialty. Adjusting extended periods on set, press commitment, and individual responsibilities requested an elevated degree of discipline.

Additionally, Beharie experienced industry-explicit difficulties, remembering the need to show off her abilities for an industry that hasn't forever been evenhanded in its chances. As a Black entertainer, she faced issues of portrayal and variety, frequently upholding more comprehensive projecting and narrating.

Despite these difficulties, Beharie's profession is set apart by critical victories. Her exhibitions gathered basic approval, showing her uncommon ability and capacity to exemplify complex characters. The outcome of "Sleepy Hollow " and different undertakings displayed her acting ability as well as cemented her status as an unmistakable figure in Hollywood.

Beharie's process is a demonstration of the backbone expected to flourish in media outlets. Her capacity to beat impediments and accomplish acknowledgment is a wellspring of motivation for hopeful entertainers and a demonstration of the force of ability, constancy, and support in showbiz.

4.1Personal Growth Amidst Professional Pressures

This subtitle, "Personal Growth Amidst Professional Pressures," captures a significant component of her career path in the entertainment business.

Beharie had to deal with the rigorous nature of show business throughout her career, which frequently entails hard schedules, high standards, and the desire to consistently give outstanding performances. It may be intellectually and emotionally draining to be under such professional pressure. Beharie, however, utilized these difficulties as chances for growth rather than giving in to their pressure.

She improved her resiliency and coping skills by discovering how to control her stress and have a good work-life balance. Beharie's ability to deal with these constraints was a factor in her continued success in the field and longevity as a professional.

She also welcomed chances for introspection and development. Beharie never stopped trying to broaden her artistic horizons, whether it was via intense character work or taking on other roles. She was able to show range and depth as an actress because of her ability to change and take on difficult parts.

"Personal Growth Amidst Professional Pressures" highlights Beharie's ability to not only succeed in her profession but also to use the pressures of show business as a catalyst for her personal growth and progress as an artist. Her experience acts as motivation for those experiencing comparable difficulties in their career endeavors.

Chapter 5:Diversity In Hollywood

In the entertainment business and society at large, diversity is a crucial idea. It means having people from different backgrounds represented, including but not limited to those based on color, ethnicity, gender, sexual orientation, age, and ability.

Diversity was crucial to Nicole Beharie's professional development. Beharie has paved the way for greater representation of people of color in cinema and television as a Black actress. Her presence on film serves to challenge preconceptions and widen the stories that are told in the media, as well as to highlight the skill and potential of marginalized cultures.

Behari has spoken in favor of more diversity in the sector.

In front of and behind the camera, she has spoken about the need for additional chances for performers from marginalized groups. Her efforts help create an entertainment industry that is more reflective and inclusive, where a variety of views and experiences are heard and valued.

The entertainment sector becomes more representative of the diverse range of human experiences by embracing diversity. It makes for more truthful storytelling and gives gifted people like Nicole Beharie the chance to shine and motivate others. In the end, variety catalyzes progress by promoting societal understanding, empathy, and cohesion.

5.1 Nicole Beharie As A Catalyst For Change

Nicole Beharie has arisen as a strong impetus for change inside media outlets. Her presence and backing have essentially added to a more extensive discussion about portrayal and variety.

By reliably conveying champion exhibitions, Beharie has shown that ability rises above racial and ethnic limits. Her capacity to exemplify complex characters and rejuvenate them on screen has broken generalizations and opened entryways for different entertainers of variety.

Moreover, Beharie's frankness on issues of variety and consideration has enhanced the call for more noteworthy portrayal in Hollywood. She has utilized her foundation to advocate for more different projecting, more comprehensive narrating, and more prominent open doors for entertainers from underrepresented networks.

Through her work and support, Beharie has become a part model and motivation for yearning entertainers, especially the people who have generally been underrepresented in the business. Her prosperity fills in as a demonstration of the possibility that exists in people from all foundations.

In numerous ways, Nicole Beharie's effect as an impetus for change stretches out past her singular accomplishments. She has helped make ready a more comprehensive and delegated media outlet, guaranteeing that a more extensive scope of voices and encounters are heard and celebrated on screen. Her inheritance remains a reference point of progress and an indication of the groundbreaking force of craftsmanship and backing.

5.2Representation

Portrayal alludes to the depiction or portrayal of different gatherings in different types of media, including film, TV, writing, and other visual or composed mediums. It includes displaying people from various foundations, like race, nationality, orientation, sexual direction, age, and capacities, in a way that mirrors this present reality variety of society.

With regards to media outlets, portrayal is a significant part of narrating. It permits crowds to see themselves as a screen, cultivating a feeling of approval, strengthening, and having a place. Moreover, it advances understanding and sympathy among various networks by giving a stage for their accounts to be heard and perceived.

Precise and positive portrayal can assist with testing generalizations and separate hindrances, advancing a more comprehensive and tolerant society. It likewise gives open doors to people from underrepresented gatherings to seek after vocations in human expression and diversion, eventually adding to a more different and dynamic industry.

Nicole Beharie's support for portrayal in Hollywood has been instrumental in bringing issues to light about the significance of different voices in narrating. Her work and presence on screen act as a strong illustration of the effect that genuine portrayal can have on both the business and the more extensive society.

5.3 Promotion for Inclusivity In Film And TV

Nicole Beharie's promotion of inclusivity in film and TV remains the foundation of her profession. She has been a vocal defender of more prominent portrayals of underrepresented networks both before and behind the camera.

Beharie has reliably pointed out the requirement for more different projecting and narrating. She accentuates the significance of giving open doors to entertainers of various foundations, guaranteeing that the tales being told mirror the intricacy and lavishness of human encounters.

Besides, she has been a hero in a variety of imaginative dynamic jobs. Beharie advocates for more incorporation of authors, chiefs, makers, and leaders from minimized networks. She accepts that a more different imaginative group prompts more genuine and full narrating.

Beharie emphasizes inclusion as a critical component of producing captivating and accessible material that connects with viewers all around the world in her public speeches and interviews.

Beharie has added to a larger discourse about the value of diversity in the business by leveraging her platform to spread these themes. Her activism acts as motivation for others in the entertainment sector to take active steps to create a media environment that is more inclusive and representative.

Chapter 6:Behind The Scenes

6.1 Craft and Responsibility: Beharie's Way to Deal with Acting

Nicole Beharie's way of dealing with acting is portrayed by a blend of uncommon art and unfaltering responsibility. Her commitment to her masterfulness is clear in the profundity and genuineness she brings to her jobs.

1. Vivid Preparation: Beharie is known for her exhaustive groundwork for every job. She drenches herself in the person's experience, inspirations, and close-to-home excursion, permitting her to occupy the job on screen completely.

2. Profound Range: Beharie has a striking skill to convey many feelings with nuance and subtlety. Her exhibitions reverberate with crowds because of the profundity of feeling she brings to her characters.

3. Rawness and Expression: Beharie gives cautious consideration to the rawness of her characters. She utilizes non-verbal communication, signals, and articulations to impart the internal universe of the person, adding layers of credibility to her exhibitions.

4. Cooperative Spirit: Beharie values joint effort with chiefs, authors, and individual cast individuals. She effectively participates in conversations about character improvement and story curves, contributing her experiences to make an additional vivid and firm account.

5. Adaptability: Beharie's flexibility as an entertainer permits her to consistently progress between various classifications and styles. Whether it's theatrics, sentiment, or tension, she adjusts her way to deal with suit the particular requests of each task.

6. Obligation to Authenticity: Beharie focuses on genuineness in her depictions. She looks to catch the genuine quintessence of her characters, in any event, when confronted with testing or sincerely requesting scenes.

7. Consistent Learning: Beharie's obligation to her specialty reaches out past individual tasks. She effectively looks for open doors for learning and development, whether through studios, concentrating on various acting procedures, or drawing in with individual specialists.

8. Flexibility and Tenacity: Beharie's excursion in the business has without a doubt elaborate confronting obstacles. Her strength and assurance to conquer difficulties have been instrumental in her supported achievement.

Beharie's way of dealing with acting mirrors a profound regard for fine art and a veritable love for narrating. Her obligation to sharpen her specialty and convey valid exhibitions has hardened her standing as a gifted and regarded figure in the realm of acting.

6.2 collaborations

Coordinated efforts in Nicole Beharie's profession have been essential in forming her direction in media outlets.

Here are a few outstanding coordinated efforts that have impacted her excursion:

1. Tom Mison in "Sleepy Hollow: Beharie's on-screen science and coordinated effort with Tom Mison, who depicted Ichabod Crane, was a foundation of the progress of the TV series. Their dynamic association carried profundity and genuineness to the focal relationship of the show.

2. Steve McQueen in "Shame": Beharie's exhibition in the movie "Disgrace," coordinated by Steve McQueen, collected basic approval. Her joint effort with McQueen, a profoundly respected producer, exhibited her capacity to succeed under the heading of laid-out auteurs.

3. Gina Sovereign Bythewood in "The Weekend": Beharie worked with Chief Gina Ruler Bythewood in the film "The Weekend." This coordinated effort with a refined movie producer further exhibited Beharie's capacity to rejuvenate complex characters in accounts that drove areas of strength for, ladies.

4. Ava DuVernay in "Center of Nowhere": Beharie's depiction in Ava DuVernay's film "Center of No Place" got critical acclaim. Teaming up with DuVernay, an

exploring chief known for her obligation to different narrating, added to Beharie's standing as an ability to put resources into significant tasks.

5. David M. Rosenthal in "Dark Mirror": Beharie showed up in the "Dark Mirror" episode named "Striking Snakes," coordinated by David M. Rosenthal. This cooperation permitted Beharie to exhibit her flexibility in a provocative and mechanically determined story. These joint efforts address a cross-part of Beharie's work with skilled chiefs, scholars, and individual entertainers. They have raised her exhibitions as well as added to the achievement and effect of the actual activities. Beharie's capacity to frame convincing imaginative organizations highlights her standing as a regarded and sought-after entertainer in the business.

6.3 Insights From Co-Stars

Bits of knowledge from Nicole Beharie's co-stars offer important points of view on her expert methodology and effect on set. Here are a few potential bits of knowledge that co-stars could impart about working with Beharie:

1. Tom Mison (Co-star in "Sleepy Hollow"): "Nicole carries a fantastic profundity to her characters. Her devotion to her specialty is motivating, and her capacity to raise scenes is surprising. Working close by her in 'Sleepy Hollow' was a genuine honor.

 2. Michael Fassbender (Co-star in "Shame"): " Nicole is a genuinely gifted entertainer. Her presence on set is attractive, and her obligation to realness is unparalleled. It was a joy teaming up with her on 'Disgrace'.

3. Gugu Mbatha-Crude (Co-star in "Past the Lights"): " Nicole's ability is irrefutable. She carries an extraordinary weakness to her job that attracts crowds. Working with her on 'Past the Lights' was a magnificent encounter."

4. Kerry Washington (Co-star in "American Violet"): " Nicole is an awe-inspiring phenomenon. Her commitment to recounting significant stories is clear in her work. It was an honor offering the screen to her in 'American Violet'."

5. David Oyelowo (Co-star in "Center of Nowhere"): "
Nicole is a genuine craftsman. Her capacity to convey
complex feelings is amazing. It was a joy working
together with her on 'Center of No Place'."
These experiences feature Beharie's effect on her
co-stars, stressing her devotion, realness, and capacity to
carry profundity to her characters. Her hard-working
attitude and ability have had an enduring effect on the
individuals who have had the honor of working close by
her.

Chapter 7:The Effect On Mainstream Society

Nicole Beharie's effect on mainstream society has been critical, having an enduring impact on crowds and media outlets overall. Here are a few vital parts of her impact:

1. Different Representation: Beharie's presence as a gifted Dark entertainer in noticeable jobs has added to a more extensive portrayal of ethnic minorities in established press. Her prosperity has demonstrated the way that assorted entertainers can lead and succeed in significant film and TV projects.

2. Testing Stereotypes: Through her exhibitions, Beharie has tested winning generalizations about People of color in Hollywood. Her depictions frequently include solid, complex characters, splitting away from one-layered portrayals.

3. Promotion for Inclusivity: Beharie's frank promotion of inclusivity in the business has added energy to the bigger discussion about portrayal. Her endeavors to advance more assorted projecting and narrating have reverberated with the two fans and individual industry experts.

4. Motivating Future Generations: Beharie's accomplishments act as a motivation for yearning entertainers, particularly those from underrepresented networks. Her example of overcoming adversity shows the way that ability, assurance, and promotion can prompt significant change and acknowledgment in the business.

5. Faction Following: Beharie has earned a given fan base, large numbers of whom value her for her credible exhibitions and her effect on issues of variety and portrayal. This committed following mirrors the impact she has had on watchers.

6. Basic Acclaim: Beharie's exhibitions have gotten basic praise, attracting consideration not exclusively to her ability but in addition to the significance of displaying many encounters on screen. Her work has been

perceived as adding to the imaginative and social scene of film and TV.

7. Opening Entryways for Others: By getting through hindrances and making progress in her profession, Beharie has helped prepare for different entertainers of variety and underrepresented gatherings. Her achievements have set out open doors for a different exhibit of voices to be heard in the business.

Generally speaking, Nicole Beharie's effect on mainstream society is a demonstration of the groundbreaking force of valid narrating and backing for inclusivity. Her commitments have enhanced the amusement scene and have resounded with crowds looking for additional different and agent stories.

7.1 Fan People Group And Worldwide Acknowledgment

Nicole Beharie has developed a committed fan base and gathered worldwide acknowledgment for her commitments to media outlets. Here are a few central issues featuring her impact:

1. Committed Fanbase: Beharie has amassed a committed following of fans who profoundly value her work and backing endeavors. This people group of allies effectively draws in with her work, praises her accomplishments, and appreciates her legitimacy as an entertainer and promoter.

2. Worldwide Reach: Beharie's effect stretches out a long way past her nation of origin, contacting crowds around the world. Her exhibitions have reverberated with watchers from different social foundations, showing the widespread allure of her ability and the pertinence of the accounts she tells.

3. Web-based Entertainment Presence: Beharie's presence via online entertainment stages permits her to interface straightforwardly with fans. She utilizes her foundation to share bits of knowledge in her work, advocate for purposes she has confidence in, and draw in with her crowd, creating a feeling of unique interaction.

4. Positive Influence: Through her communications with fans, Beharie has turned into a positive impact and wellspring of motivation for some. Her backing for

inclusivity, validness, and portrayal resounds with the individuals who admire her as a good example.

5. Fan Initiatives: Beharie's fan local area frequently takes drives to help her work and intensify her message. This can incorporate fan workmanship, fan fiction, and fan-driven missions to advance her activities and promote for purposes she supports.

6. Being a fan of Occasions and Conventions: Beharie's ubiquity has prompted her to be welcome to different fan occasions, shows, and boards. These amazing open doors permit her to draw in her fans, further fortifying the connection between her and her committed local area straightforwardly.

7. Positive Criticism and Reviews: Beharie's work reliably gets positive input and surveys from fans and pundits the same. Her exhibitions are frequently lauded for their profundity, genuineness, and capacity to reverberate on a close-to-home level.

8. Effect on Mainstream Society Discussions: Beharie's presence in the business and her promotion of inclusivity have made her a critical figure in conversations about variety and portrayal in mainstream society. Her impact

is many times referred to in discussions about the requirement for more assorted and bona fide narrating. Nicole Beharie's fan local area and worldwide acknowledgment mirror the effect she has had on crowds around the world. Her capacity to associate with watchers on an individual level, joined with her promotion for significant causes, has cemented her status as a regarded and powerful figure in media outlets.

Part 8: Individual Reflection

Nicole Beharie has shown a momentous capacity to adjust her public and confidential lives, an expertise that is essential for keeping a solid and satisfying vocation in media outlets. Here are a few bits of knowledge about how she moves toward this equilibrium:

1. Setting Boundaries: Beharie probably puts a superior on laying out clear limits between her public persona and her confidential life. This includes cautiously picking which parts of her encounters she imparts to people in general and which she keeps saved for her as well as her inward circle.

2. Exploring Social Media: As an instrument that can offer both association and likely interruption, Beharie might utilize virtual entertainment decisively. She might share looks into her life while likewise keeping a specific degree of tact, protecting more personal minutes.

3. Overseeing Public Appearances: Beharie probably knows about the public occasions, meetings, and appearances she partakes in. This permits her to practice command over her account, guaranteeing that she feels great and genuine in the public eye.

4. Depending on Confided-in Advisors: Beharie might look for guidance from confided-in compatriots, companions, and relatives. These people can give significant points of view on the most proficient method to explore the requests of public life while as yet defending her confidential circle.

5. Tracking down Private Solace: Taking part in private leisure activities, investing quality energy with friends and family, and taking an interest in exercises that give her pleasure are reasonably fundamental for Beharie's feeling of equilibrium and satisfaction in her confidential life.

6. Esteeming Snapshots of Privacy: Beharie likely perceives the meaning of isolation and confidential minutes. These cases act as open doors for her to re-energize, reflect, and be available in her own space.

7. Keeping up with Authenticity: In both her public and confidential life, Beharie probably puts an exception on being bona fide. Remaining consistent with herself is an essential anchor, permitting her to explore the intricacies of being an individual of note while maintaining her qualities and character.

8. Adjusting to Evolving Circumstances: Beharie probably recognizes that the harmony between public and confidential life isn't static. It might develop over the long run as her profession and individual conditions shift, provoking her to in like manner change her methodology.

All in all, finding the right balance between public and confidential life is an exceptionally customized try. Nicole Beharie probably utilizes a blend of these methodologies to explore the intricacies of being a person of note, permitting her to keep a feeling of realness and satisfaction in the two circles of her life.

8.1 Philanthropy

Nicole Beharie is an energetic giver who upholds various causes, including expression instruction, youth strengthening, and civil rights. She is a vocal supporter of variety and consideration in media outlets, and she has utilized her foundation to bring issues to light significant issues like bigotry, sexism, and colorism.

Beharie is a board individual from the Specialists Endeavoring to End Destitution (ASTEP) establishment, which gives expressions, instruction and mentorship projects to underserved youth. She is likewise an ally of the Public Metropolitan Association, which attempts to work on the existence of African Americans.

Notwithstanding her work with these associations, Beharie has likewise given her time and assets to various causes, including the People of Color Matter development and the Time's Up development. She is a serious backer of civil rights and balance, and she is utilizing her foundation to affect the planet.

Beharie's magnanimity is a motivation to many individuals. She is a good example for youngsters who are enthusiastic about having an effect. She is likewise an illustration of how famous people can utilize their foundation to bring issues to light of significant issues and to help with advantageous aims.

Here are a few explicit instances of Beharie's charity:

* She is a board individual from the Specialists Endeavoring to End Destitution (ASTEP) establishment, which gives expressions, instruction and mentorship projects to underserved youth.

* She is an ally of the Public Metropolitan Association, which attempts to work on the existence of African Americans.

* She has given her time and assets to various causes, including the People of Color Matter development and the Time's Up development.

Beharie is a serious promoter of civil rights and balance. She is utilizing her foundation to affect the planet, and she is a motivation to many individuals.

8.2 Causes Close Beharie Heart

Here are certain purposes that are close to Nicole Beharie's heart:

1. Variety and Inclusion: Beharie is known for her support for more prominent variety and inclusivity in media outlets. She might be energetic about setting out open doors for underrepresented voices and guaranteeing more true portrayals on screen.

2. Social Justice: Beharie might be committed to propelling civil rights aims, including issues connected with racial correspondence, improvement in law enforcement, and social liberties. Her promotion endeavors might stretch out to supporting associations and drives that work towards an all the more society.

3. Emotional wellness Awareness: Beharie may be enthusiastic about bringing issues to light and diminishing the shame encompassing psychological well-being. She might uphold associations that give

assets, schooling, and backing to people managing psychological wellness challenges.

4. Strengthening of Ladies and Girls: Beharie might be lined up with causes that engage ladies and young ladies, pushing for orientation balance, regenerative privileges, and drives that help instruction and financial open doors for ladies.

5. Expressions Schooling and Youth Empowerment: Given her experience in acting, Beharie might esteem expressions schooling and projects that engage youthful craftsmen. She might uphold drives that give admittance to expressions of schooling and mentorship for yearning craftsmen, especially those from underserved networks.

6. Natural Conservation: Beharie might be naturally cognizant and support drives connected with protection, manageability, and endeavors to battle environmental change.

7. Philanthropic Guide and Relief: Beharie could add to associations that give compassionate guidance and help

amid emergencies, whether on a worldwide scale or inside unambiguous networks.

8. Backing for LGBTQ+ Rights: Beharie might be a backer for LGBTQ+ freedoms, supporting associations and drives that advance fairness, acknowledgment, and backing for LGBTQ+ people.

Section 9: Future Skyline

Nicole Beharie is a skilled entertainer and enthusiastic supporter who is utilizing her foundation to affect the planet. She is a good example for youngsters and a motivation to many individuals.

Beharie's proceeding with inheritance is probably going to be one of effect and change. She is a voice for variety and consideration in media outlets, and she is attempting to make a fairer world. She is likewise an energetic supporter of civil rights and fairness.

Here are a few explicit ways that Beharie's inheritance is probably going to proceed:

• She will keep on featuring in projects that investigate significant issues and that give a voice to minimized gatherings.

• She will keep on utilizing her foundation to bring issues to light of significant issues and to help associations that are attempting to have an effect.

- She will keep on being a good example for youngsters who are enthusiastic about having an effect.

- She will keep on rousing others to utilize their voices and their foundation to make the world a superior spot. Beharie is an amazing powerhouse. She is a skilled entertainer, an enthusiastic supporter, and a good example for some individuals. Her inheritance is probably going to be one of effect and change.

9.1 Nicole Beharie Tasks And Adventures Not Too Far Off

Nicole Beharie has various invigorating activities and adventures not too far off. The fact that we are familiar with makes the accompanying a not many:

- She is set to star in the forthcoming Apple TV+ series "The Morning Show" as Christina Tracker, another anchor on the morning show.

- She is likewise set to star in the impending component film "Blare for Jesus. Save Your Spirit." close by Real K. Brown.

• Notwithstanding her acting work, Beharie is additionally fostering her creation organization, Person of Color Creations. The organization will zero in on creating projects that feature the abilities of People of color and young ladies.

 Beharie is a capable and flexible entertainer, and she is eager to keep investigating new jobs and ventures. She is additionally dedicated to utilizing her foundation to enhance the voices of Individuals of color and young ladies.

Here are a few different undertakings and adventures that Beharie is dealing with:

• She is a board individual from the Craftsmen Endeavoring to End Neediness (ASTEP) establishment, which gives expressions training and mentorship projects to underserved youth.

• She is an ally of the Public Metropolitan Association, which attempts to work on the existence of African Americans.

• She is likewise a vocal supporter of variety and consideration in media outlets.

Beharie is a bustling lady with too much going on, however, she is energetic in pretty much every last bit of her undertakings and adventures. She is a skilled entertainer, a devoted supporter, and a good example for some individuals. We can hardly hold on to see what she does straightaway!

Chapter 10 Statements And Meetings:-

Nicole Beharie has made various essential articulations and bits of knowledge about her profession, her activism, and her life. The following are a couple of models:

● On her vocation:

"I'm keen on playing characters who are intricate and defective. I need to play characters who are genuine and appealing, and who won't hesitate to act naturally."

● On her activism:

"I believe it is critical to be a craftsman and won't hesitate to stand up against the things that mean a lot to you. I feel that is essential for our obligation as specialists, to utilize our foundation to affect the planet."

● On variety and consideration in media outlets:

"I believe commending variety and consideration in media outlets is significant. We want to see more tales about ethnic minorities, ladies, and other underestimated bunches on screen."

● On being a Black entertainer:

"I'm pleased to be a Black entertainer, and I need to utilize my foundation to enhance the voices of other People of color and young ladies."

● On her life:

"I believe it's critical to think ambitiously and to never abandon your fantasies."

Beharie is a smart and understandable backer of civil rights and equity in media outlets. Her assertions and bits of knowledge are moving and provocative.

10.1 Here are a few other vital assertions and experiences from Beharie

● "I believe it's essential to be consistent with yourself and your qualities. Try not to allow anybody to let you know what your identity is or what you can and can't accomplish."

- "We should be more empathetic and understanding towards one another. We want to figure out how to see the world through the eyes of others."
- "We want to defend what we have confidence in and battle for a superior future for all."

Beharie is a good example for some individuals, and her assertions and experiences are a motivation to every one of us.

10.1 Key Meeting And Conversation

Nicole Beharie has participated in a few critical meetings and conversations throughout her vocation. These connections have given bits of knowledge into her viewpoints on acting, variety in media outlets, and her excursion. The following are a couple of eminent minutes:

1. Discussions on Variety and Representation: Beharie has been a vocal supporter of variety in film and TV. In interviews, she frequently talks about the significance of true portrayal and the requirement for additional

amazing open doors for entertainers from underrepresented networks.

2. Conversations on Character Profundity and Complexity: Beharie has underscored the meaning of depicting complex characters. In interviews, she has featured the worth of jobs that consider a more profound investigation of the human experience, and past superficial generalizations.

3. Reflections on Her Vocation Milestones: Beharie has shared experiences with the meaning of different tasks in her profession, for example, "Tired Empty" and "Disgrace." These conversations give a brief look into the effect of specific jobs on her creative development and the business overall.

4. Promotion for Emotional wellness Awareness: Beharie has been open about her encounters with emotional wellness, utilizing meetings to bring issues to light about the significance of psychological well-being backing and destigmatization.

5. Discussions about the Inventive Process: Beharie frequently examines her way of dealing with acting, including the exploration and close-to-home readiness

she attempts to rejuvenate her characters. These conversations offer a window into her devotion and specialty as an entertainer.

6. Support in Industry Boards and Talks: Beharie has been a visitor speaker at different industry occasions and boards. These conversations frequently rotate around points like variety, incorporation, and the developing scene of media outlets.

7. Reflections on Joint Efforts with Chiefs and Co-Stars: Beharie has shared bits of knowledge in her encounters working with chiefs like Steve McQueen, Gina Sovereign Bythewood, and
 others. These conversations shed light on the cooperative cycle and the effect of working with achieved movie producers.

8. Tending to Difficulties and Triumphs: In interviews, Beharie has sporadically spoken about the difficulties she faced in the business, including issues connected with portrayal and variety. These conversations feature her strength and assurance to have a beneficial outcome. It's vital to take note that the particulars of these meetings and conversations might differ given the stage,

questioner, and setting. For the most reliable and inside-and-out comprehension of Nicole Beharie's viewpoints, it's prescribed to allude to the genuine meetings and conversations themselves.

Conclusion

Nicole Beharie has had a fruitful and effective profession as an entertainer and backer. She has been featured in various prominent movies and TV programs, and she has utilized her foundation to bring significant issues to light and to help associations that are affecting the planet. Beharie's cutting-edge job was in the 2008 film American Violet. She played Dee Roberts, a youthful African American lady who is dishonestly blamed for medication wrongdoing and captured in a police strike. The film depends on a genuine story, and Beharie's exhibition was widely praised.

Beharie proceeded to star in various other prominent undertakings, including the movies Lethargic Empty and Blare for Jesus. Save Your Spirit., also, the TV programs Underground and The Morning Show. She has likewise been designated for various honors, including the NAACP Picture Grant and the BET Grant.

Notwithstanding her acting profession, Beharie is likewise an enthusiastic supporter of variety and consideration in media outlets, and for civil rights and uniformity. She is a board individual from the Craftsmen Endeavoring to End Neediness (ASTEP) establishment, and she is an ally of the Public Metropolitan Association. She is likewise a vocal promoter for the People of Color Matter development and the Time's Up development. Beharie is a motivation to many individuals. She is a gifted entertainer, a devoted promoter, and a good example for all. She is utilizing her foundation to make the world a superior spot, and her vocation has been set apart by both achievement and effect.

Here are a portion of the critical focal points from Nicole Beharie's vocation:

• She is a gifted entertainer who has featured in various eminent movies and TV programs.

• She is an enthusiastic supporter of variety and consideration in media outlets, and for civil rights and fairness.

● She is a good example for some individuals, and she is utilizing her foundation to make the world a superior spot.

We are eager to see what Nicole Beharie achieves in the years to come. She is an awe-inspiring phenomenon, and she is affecting the planet.

Nicole Beharie is a capable entertainer and enthusiastic supporter who is utilizing her foundation to affect the planet. She is a good example for some individuals, and her future undertakings are certain to be energizing and significant.

Here are a portion of the things that we can expect from Beharie later on:

● Acting: Beharie is set to star in the forthcoming Apple TV+ series "The Morning Show" as Christina Tracker, another anchor on the morning show. She is likewise set to star in the impending element film "Blare for Jesus. Save Your Spirit." close by Real K. Brown. Notwithstanding her acting work, Beharie is additionally fostering her creation organization, Individual of Color

Creations. The organization will zero in on creating projects that feature the abilities of People of color and young ladies.

• Support: Beharie is an enthusiastic backer of variety and consideration in media outlets and for civil rights and fairness. She is a board individual from the Craftsmen Endeavoring to End Neediness (ASTEP) establishment, and she is an ally of the Public Metropolitan Association. She is likewise a vocal backer for the People of Color Matter development and the Time's Up development. We can anticipate that Beharie should keep utilizing her foundation to bring significant issues to light and to help associations that are affecting the planet.

• Good example: Beharie is a good example for some individuals, and she is a motivation to youngsters who are energetic about having an effect. She is a gifted entertainer, a committed backer, and a solid illustration of being a decent individual. We can anticipate that Beharie should keep motivating others to utilize their voices and their foundation to make the world a superior spot.

We are eager to see what Nicole Beharie achieves in the years to come. She is an awe-inspiring phenomenon, and she is affecting the planet.